JOURNEYS

Program Consultants

Shervaughnna Anderson · Marty Hougen
Carol Jago · Erik Palmer · Shane Templeton
Sheila Valencia · MaryEllen Vogt

Consulting Author · Irene Fountas

Cover illustration by Scott Nash.

Printed in the U.S.A.

ISBN   978-0-544-54326-3

14 15 16   0690   23 22 21 20 19
4500752845   BCDEFG

Unit 1

Unit 2

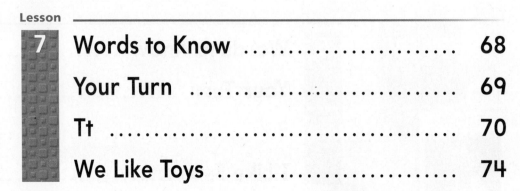

4

Unit 3

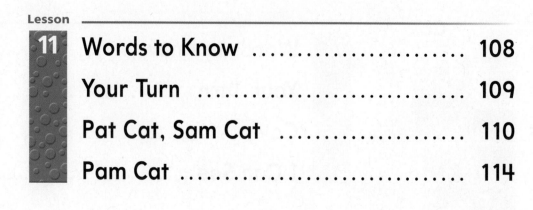

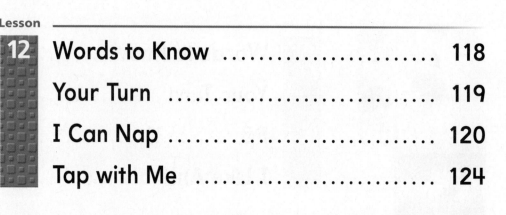

6

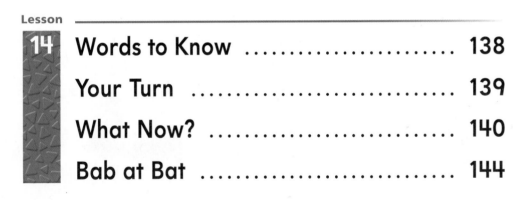

WORDS TO KNOW

High-Frequency Words

I

Vocabulary Reader

Context Cards

I have a big family!

Words to Know

Read Together

▸ Read the word.

▸ Talk about the picture.

I

I have a big family!

Your Turn

Talk About It!

Families are different. What is the same about all families? Share ideas with a partner.

See What We Can Do

by Susan Gorman-Howe

illustrated by Sue Dennen

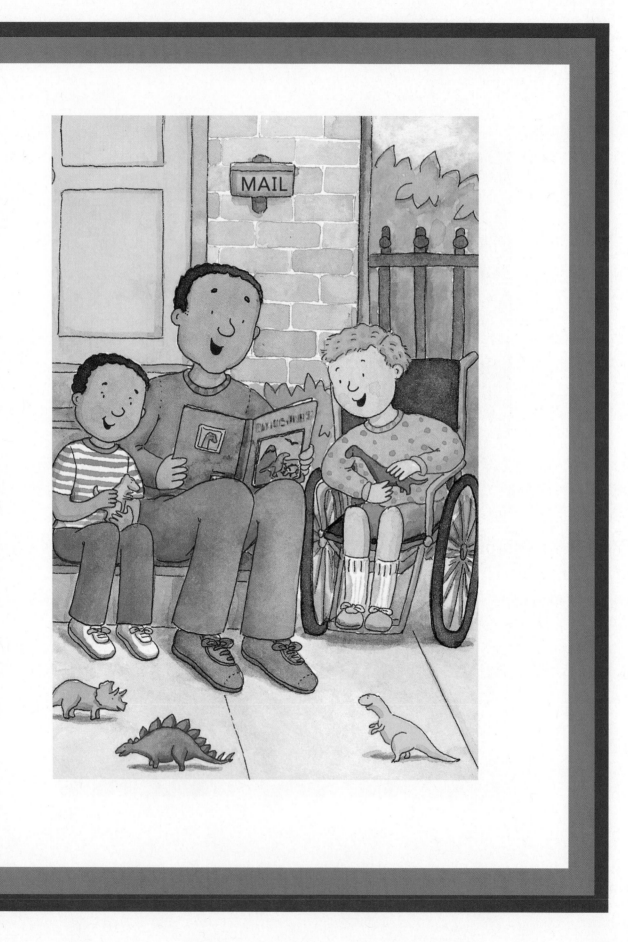

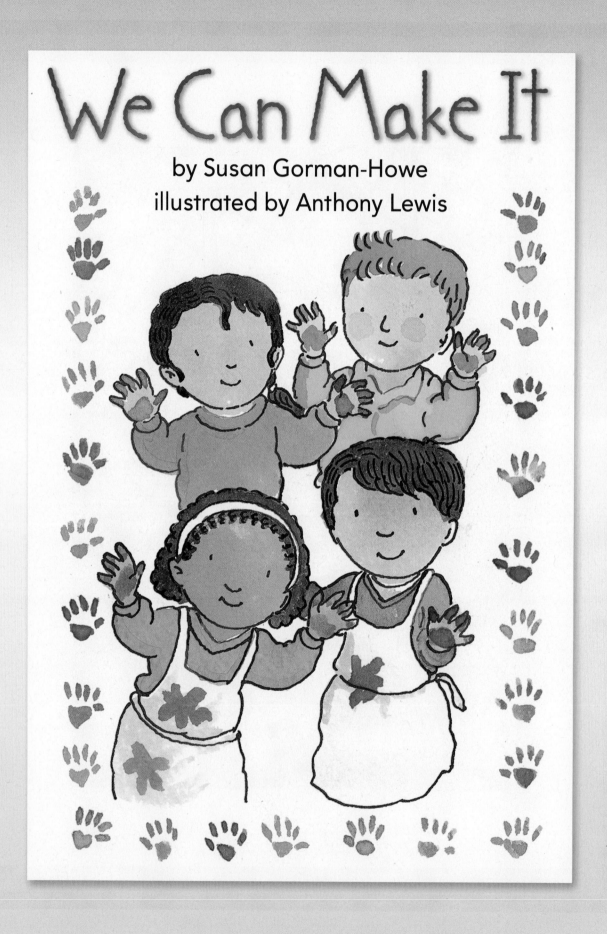

We Can Make It

by Susan Gorman-Howe

illustrated by Anthony Lewis

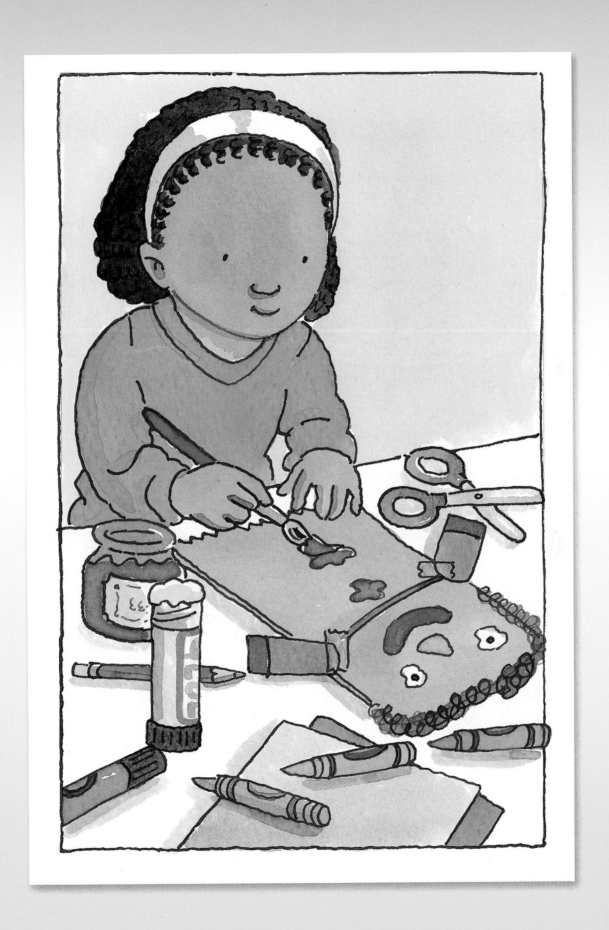

We Go to School
by Susan Garman-Howe
illustrated by Maryann Cocca-Leffler

I Like
by Owen Marcus
illustrated by Maribel Suarez

WORDS TO KNOW

High-Frequency Words

like

Vocabulary
Reader

At School
by Philip Rush

Context
Cards

We like to go to school!

ELA RL.K.1, RF.K.3c, SL.K.2

18

Words to Know

Read
Together

▶ Read the word.

▶ Talk about the picture.

like

We like to go to school!

Your Turn

Talk About It!

Talk about what happens when the dinosaurs do not follow the rules. Why do we have rules at school?

We Go to School

by Susan Gorman-Howe

illustrated by Maryann Cocca-Leffler

I Like

by Owen Marcus

illustrated by Maribel Suarez

I like  .

I like .

I like .

I like  .

Baby Bear's Family
by Susan Garman-Howe
illustrated by Angela Jarecki

The Party
by Ron Kingsley
illustrated by Yvette Banek

WORDS TO KNOW
High-Frequency Words

the

Vocabulary
Reader

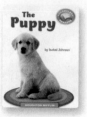

The Puppy
by Isabel Johnson

Context
Cards

ELA RL.K.3, RF.K.3c, SL.K.2

Words to Know

Read Together

▸ Read the word.

▸ Talk about the picture.

the

Do you see the puppy?

Your Turn

Talk About It!

Talk to a friend. Tell why pets need someone to take care of them.

Baby Bear's Family

by Susan Gorman-Howe

illustrated by Angela Jarecki

The Party

by Ron Kingsley

illustrated by Yvette Banek

I like the .

I like the .

I like the .

I like the .

WORDS TO KNOW
High-Frequency Words

and

Vocabulary
Reader

Context
Cards

Words to Know

Read
Together

▸ Read the word.

▸ Talk about the picture.

and

A worker has a saw and a hammer.

Your Turn

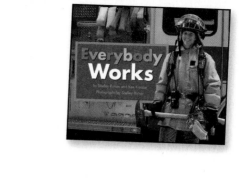

Talk About It!

What kinds of work do people do?   Tell a partner.

Mm

by Pat Macnan

illustrated by
Diana Schoenbrun

Mm

I Like Mm

by Pat Macnan

I like the .

I like the .

Mm

I like the 🥛.

Mm

I like the 🥛 and the 🧁🧁.

WORDS TO KNOW

High-Frequency Words

I

like

Vocabulary
Reader

Context
Cards

ELA RI.K.7, RF.K.3c, SL.K.2

Words to Know

Read
Together

▶ You learned these words. Use each one in a sentence.

I

I have a big family!

like

We like to go to school!

Your Turn

Talk About It!

The Handiest Things
in the World
ANDREW CLEMENTS
Photographs by Raquel Jaramillo

How do tools help us do things with our hands?
Tell a partner what you think.

Ss

by Pat Macnan

illustrated by Diana Schoenbrun

I Like Ss

by Pablo Lopez

I like the .

I like the .

I like the ☀.

Ss

I like the  and the .

WORDS TO KNOW

High-Frequency Words

see

Vocabulary Reader

Context Cards

ELA RI.K.1, RF.K.3c, SL.K.2

Words to Know

Read Together

▸ Read the word.

▸ Talk about the picture.

see

What can you **see** in the city?

Your Turn

Talk About It!

How do you use your senses to learn about the world?   Tell a friend.

Aa

by Roberto Livingston

illustrated by Bernard Adnet

Aa

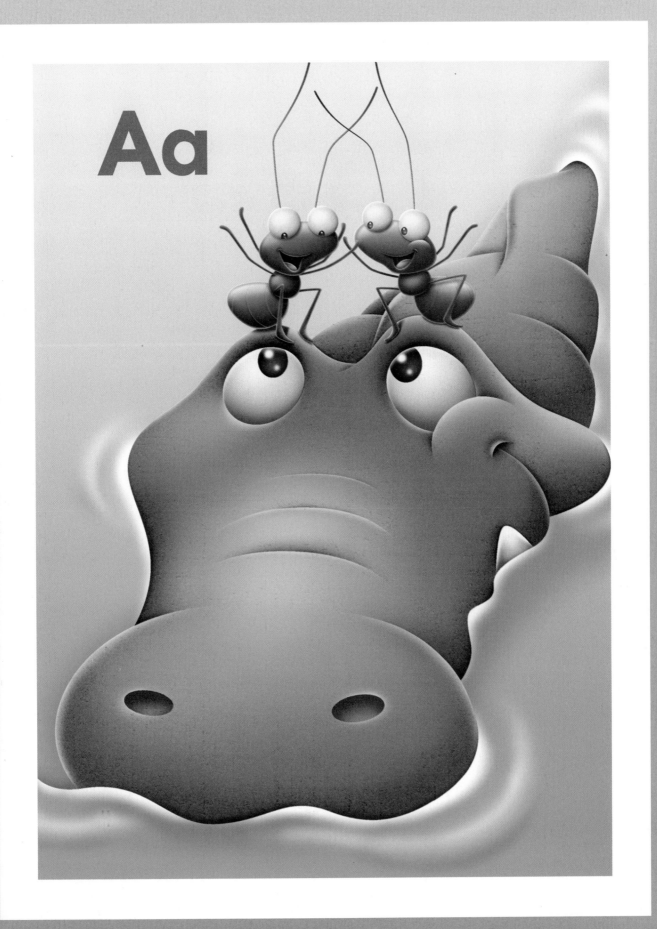

Aa

I See

by Sheila Hoffman

I see the .

Aa

I see the .

Aa

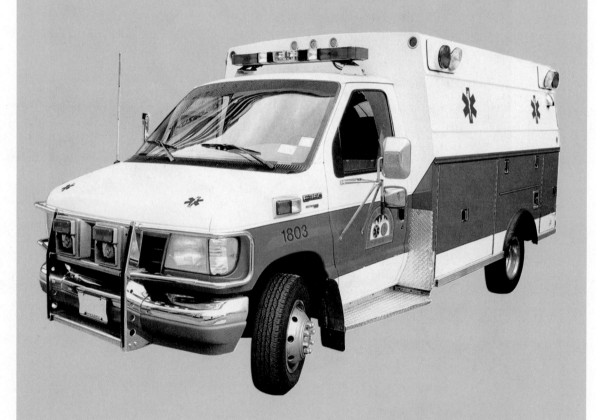

I see the .

Aa

I see the  .

WORDS TO KNOW

High-Frequency Words

we

Vocabulary Reader

Context Cards

ELA RL.K.1, RF.K.3c

Words to Know

Read Together

▶ Read the word.

▶ Talk about the picture.

we

Our cat purrs when we pet her.

Your Turn

Talk About It!

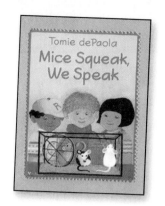

How do people and animals communicate? Talk about it with a friend. Use words from the **Big Book** as you share ideas.

Tt

by Nimesh Sing
illustrated by Priscilla Burris

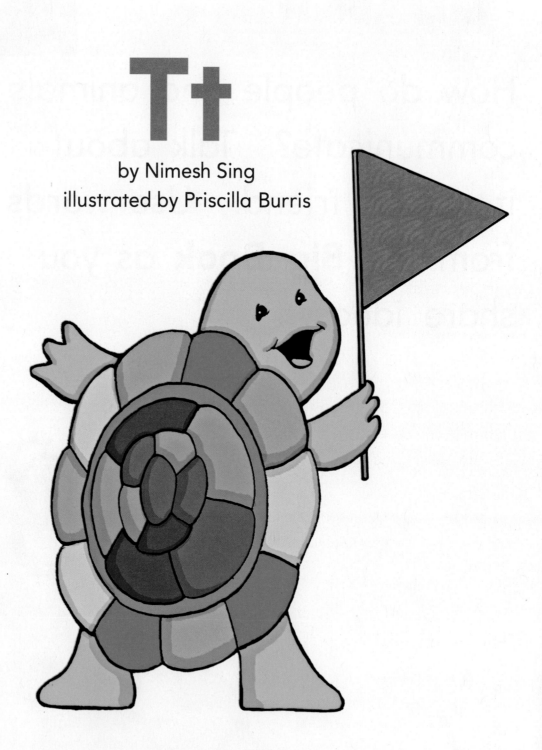

Tt

72

Tt

We Like Toys

by Matthew Lorer

Tt

I like the .

Tt

We like the 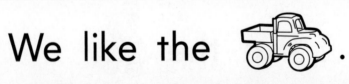.

Tt

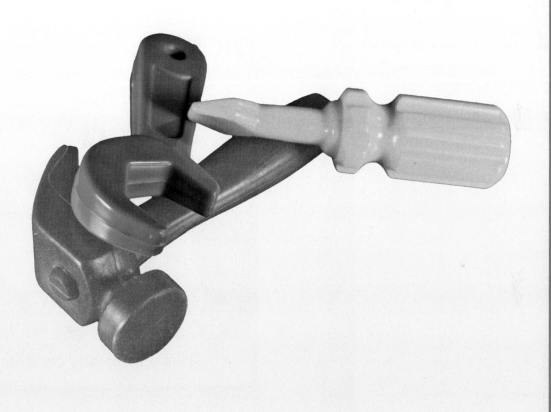

We like the 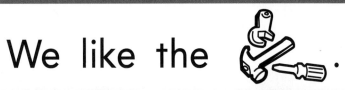 .

WORDS TO KNOW

High-Frequency Words

a

**Vocabulary
Reader**

**Context
Cards**

ELA RI.K.1, RI.K.7, RF.K.3c

Words to Know

Read Together

▸ Read the word.

▸ Talk about the picture.

a

This rabbit sits on a log.

Your Turn

Talk About It!

Move!
Steve Jenkins & Robin Page

Why do different animals move in different ways? Talk about it with a friend.

Cc

by David Ashford

illustrated by John Segal

Cc

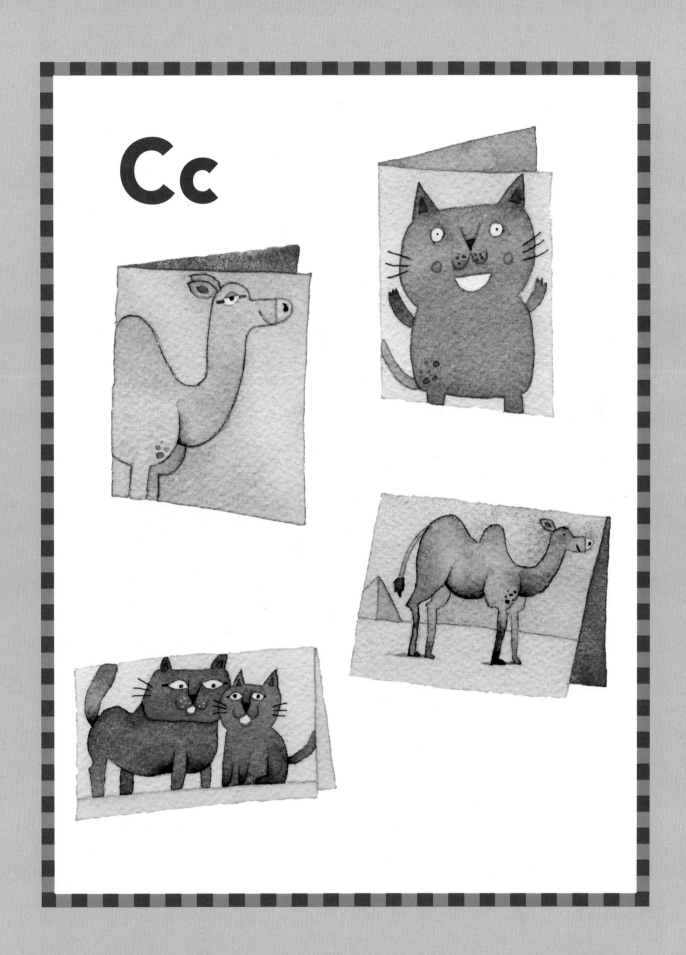

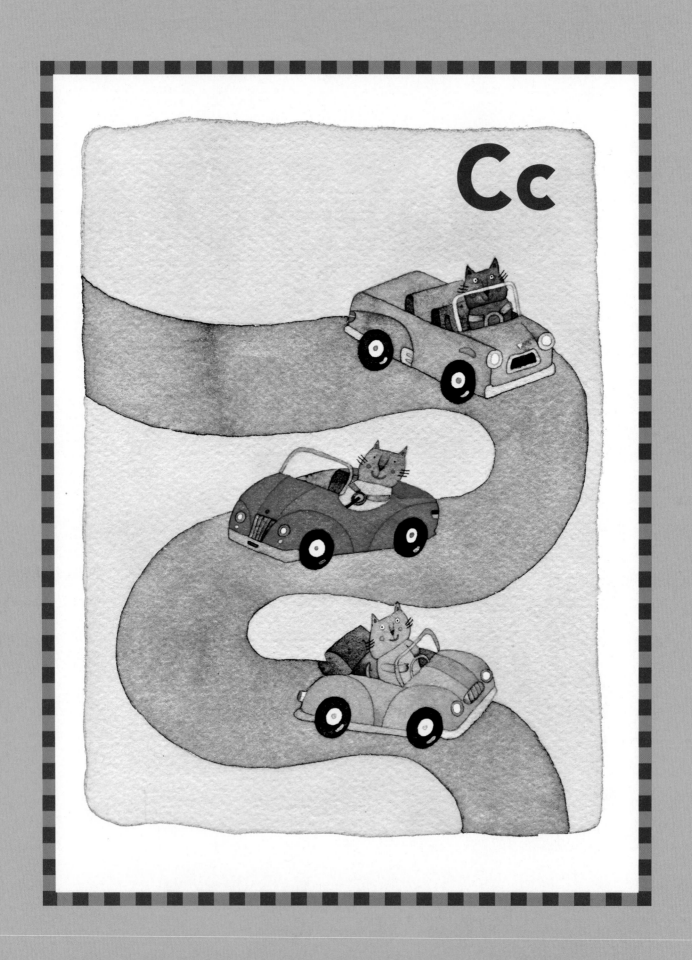

Cc

I Can See

by Laticia Craven

I see a .

Cc

I see a .

Cc

I see a  .

Cc

I see a  .

WORDS TO KNOW

High-Frequency Words

to

Vocabulary
Reader

Context
Cards

ELA RI.K.7, RF.K.3c, SL.K.2

Words to Know

Read
Together

▸ Read the word.

▸ Talk about the picture.

to

1

We like **to** ride our bikes!

Your Turn

Talk About It!

Why do people use wheels?
Talk with a partner.

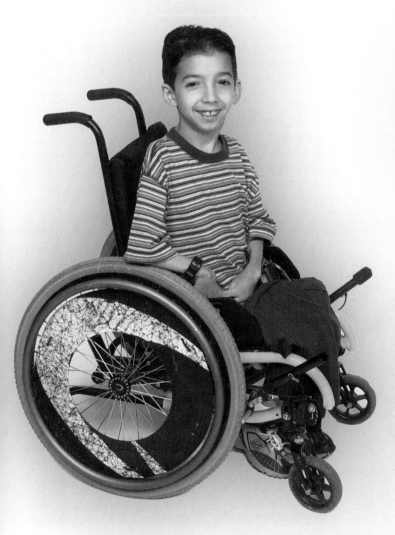

Pp

by Diondra Thomas
illustrated Kristin Sorra

Pp

Pp

I Like Animals

by Sydney Mueller

I like to see 🐖🐖 .

Pp

I like to see .

Pp

I like to see 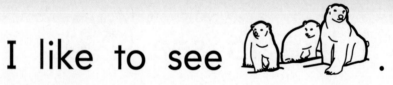 .

Pp

I like to see 🦜🦜 .

WORDS TO KNOW

High-Frequency Words

see

we

Vocabulary
Reader

Context
Cards

ELA RL.K.1, RL.K.2, RF.K.3c

98

Words [Read Together]
to Know

▶ You learned these
words. Use each
one in a sentence.

see

What can you **see** in the city?

we

Our cat purrs when **we** pet her.

Your Turn

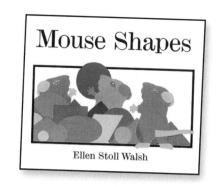

Mouse Shapes

Ellen Stoll Walsh

Talk About It!

What do the mice make with shapes in the **Big Book?** What can we create with shapes? Talk with a partner.

Mmmm, Good!

by Angela Ferie

illustrated Ana Ochoa

I see .

I like .

We like  .

We like to see .

The Playground

by Paul Falcon

illustrated by Robin Oz

I like the .

I like to  .

We see the ⌂.

We like the .

Pat Cat, Sam Cat
by Greg Kent

Pam Cat
by Louise Andreas
illustrated by Judith Lanfredi

WORDS TO KNOW
High-Frequency Words

come

me

Vocabulary
Reader

Context
Cards

Fun in July

The rain will come down in spring.

ELA RI.K.1, RI.K.10, RF.K.3c

Words to Know

Read Together

▶ Read the words.

▶ Talk about the pictures.

come

1

The rain will come down in spring.

me

2

This hat is for me.

Your Turn

Talk About It!

Jump into January
A Journey Around the Year
Stella Blackstone
Maria Carluccio

How does the weather change in different months and seasons? Talk to a friend about it.

Pat Cat, Sam Cat

by Greg Kent

Pat Cat, Pat Cat.

I am Pat Cat.

Come to me, Pat Cat!
Pat Cat sat.

Sam Cat, Sam Cat.
I am Sam Cat.

Come to me, Sam Cat!
Sam Cat sat.

Pam Cat

by Louise Andreas

illustrated by Judith Lanfredi

Pam Cat! Pam Cat! Pam Cat!

Pam Cat! Pam Cat! Pam Cat!

I see Pam Cat.
Come to me, Pam Cat.

Pam Cat sat.

Pam Cat and I sat.

I pat Pam Cat.

I pat and pat Pam Cat.

I Can Nap
by Christopher Lawrence

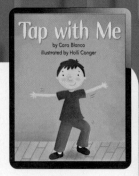

Tap with Me
by Cara Blanco
illustrated by Holli Conger

WORDS TO KNOW

High-Frequency Words

with
my

Vocabulary Reader

Animals in the Snow

Context Cards

Words to Know

Read Together

▸ Read the words.

▸ Talk about the pictures.

with

The trees are covered with snow.

my

The snowman wears my scarf.

Your Turn

Talk About It!

snow

Manya Stojic

What do animals do when the weather changes? Talk to a partner about it.

I Can Nap

by Christopher Lawrence

 can nap.

 can nap, nap, nap, nap.

I am Dan.

I can nap with my .

We can nap, nap, nap, nap.

121

 can nap.

 can nap, nap, nap, nap.

I am Pat.

I can nap with my .

We can nap, nap, nap, nap.

Tap with Me

by Cara Blanco

illustrated by Holli Conger

I can tap.
I tap, tap, tap.

I can tap. Nan can tap.
Nan can tap, tap, tap.

I can tap with Nan.
Tap, tap, tap.

I am Tap Man!
Tap, tap, tap! Tap Man!

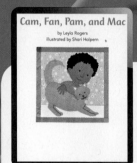

Cam, Fan, Pam, and Mac
by Leyla Rogers
illustrated by Shari Halpern

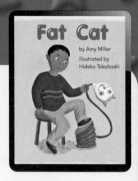

Fat Cat
by Amy Miller
illustrated by Hideko Takahashi

WORDS TO KNOW
High-Frequency Words

you

what

Vocabulary Reader

Lots of Birds

Context Cards

ELA RI.K.1, RF.K.3c, SL.K.1a

Words to Know

Read Together

▸ Read the words.

▸ Talk about the pictures.

you

1

Do you see the butterfly?

what

2

What colors do you see?

Your Turn

Talk About It!

What Do You Do With a Tail Like This?

Steve Jenkins & Robin Page

How do animals use their body parts? Talk to a partner about it.

Cam, Fan, Pam, and Mac

by Leyla Rogers

illustrated by Shari Halpern

Cam can see a tan cat.

Cam can pat the tan cat.

The fat tan cat can see Cam.

Fan can see Nat.
Can Nat see Fan?
Nat can! Nat can!

Pam can see Sam.

Sam can nap, nap, nap!

Pam sat with Sam.

What can Mac see?
Mac can see you.

Fat Cat

by Amy Miller

illustrated by
Hideko Takahashi

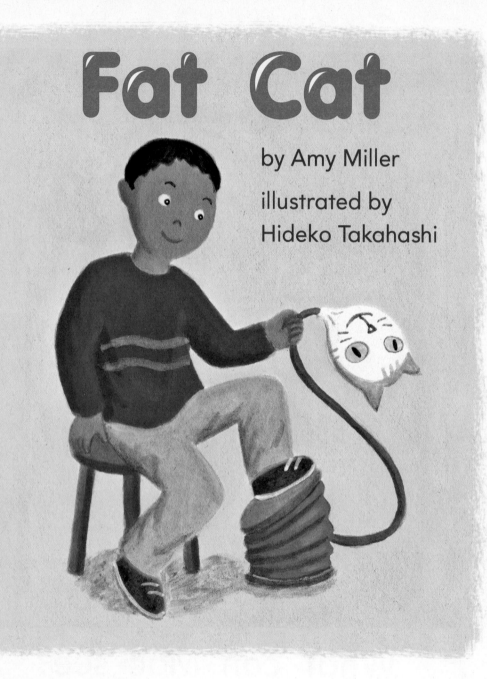

Sam sat.
Sam sat to tap, tap, tap.

Can you see the cat?

Sam can tap, tap, tap, tap.

Tap, Sam! Tap, Sam!
Tap. Tap. Tap.

Can you see the fat cat?
What a fat, fat cat!

WORDS TO KNOW
High-Frequency Words

are

now

Vocabulary
Reader

Context
Cards

ELA RF.K.3c, SL.K.2

Words to Know
Read Together

▸ Read the words.

▸ Talk about the pictures.

are

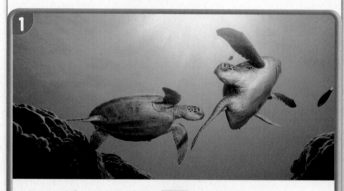

The turtles **are** swimming.

now

The turtle is sleeping **now**.

Your Turn

Talk About It!

What animals can you find near a pond? Talk to a partner about it.

139

What Now?

by Suzanne Gerardi

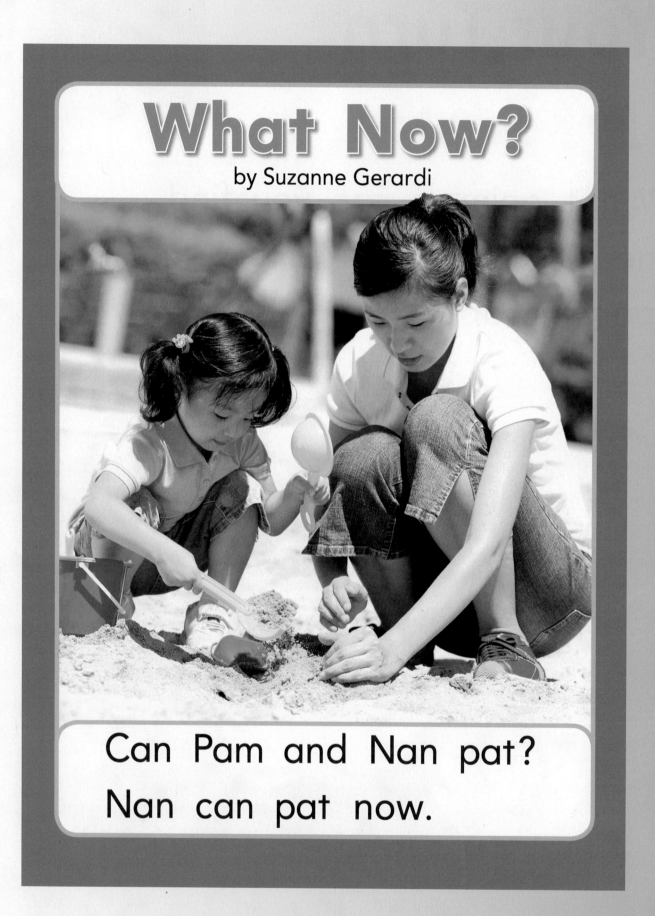

Can Pam and Nan pat?
Nan can pat now.

Can Nat tap? Nat can!
Nat can tap now.

Sam and Bab are at bat.
Can Sam bat? Sam can.
Bat, Sam, bat!

Now we can nap.

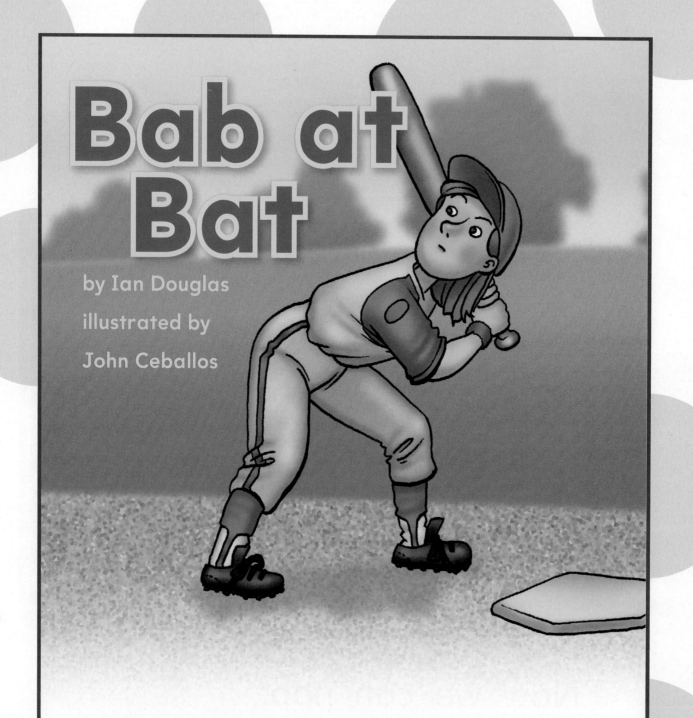

Bab at Bat

by Ian Douglas

illustrated by

John Ceballos

See Bab at bat?
Bab can bat.

Bab can bat now.
Bat, Bab! Bat!
Bam!

Bab CAN bat!
Pat can see Bab bat.
You can, Pat! You can!

Pat can. We can.
We are , Pat!

Mac and Pam Cat
by Nina Dimopolous
Illustrated by Bari Weissmann

Come with Me
by Roger DiPaulo
illustrated by Fahimeh Amiri

WORDS TO KNOW
High-Frequency Words

come

me

Vocabulary Reader

Context Cards

In the Sky
by Tamsil Morgan

The rain will come down in spring.

ELA RI.K.1, RI.K.2, RF.K.3c

Words to Know

Read Together

▶ You learned these words. Use each one in a sentence.

come

The rain will come down in spring.

me

This hat is for me.

Your Turn

Talk About It!

What can we see in the sky? Talk to a friend about it.

Your Turn

Talk About It!

What can we see in the sky? Talk to a friend about it.

Mac and Pam Cat

by Nina Dimopolous

illustrated by Bari Weissmann

Mac sat and sat.

Pam Cat sat.
Mac can pat Pam Cat.

Mac sat with Pam Cat.
Mac can fan Pam Cat.

Come to me, Pam Cat.
Pam Cat!   Pam Cat!

Come with Me

by Roger DiPaulo

illustrated by Fahimeh Amiri

Nat sat and sat.
Nat sat, sat, sat.

Come with me, Bab!
Bab! Bab! Bab!

Nat sat. Bab sat.
Nat can see Nan.
Bab can see Nan.

Nat sat. Bab sat. Nan sat.

Unit 1

● ● ● ● ● ● ● ● ● ● ● ● ● ● ● ●

Lesson 1

See What We Can Do	We Can Make It
Wordless Story	Wordless Story

Lesson 2

We Go to School	I Like
Wordless Story	High-Frequency Words
	I, like

Lesson 3

Baby Bear's Family	The Party
Wordless Story	High-Frequency Words
	I, like, the

Lesson 4

Mm	I Like Mm	
Suggested Words	Suggested Words	High-Frequency Words
masks, mice, mittens, moon, mountains, mouse, music	milk, moon, mouse, muffins	and, I, like, the

158

Lesson		
5	**Ss**	**I Like Ss**
	Suggested Words	Suggested Words / High-Frequency Words
	sailboat, sailing, sailor, sea, seal, soccer, sun, surf, surfboard	sailboat, sandwich, seal, soup, sun and, I, like, the

Unit 2

Lesson		
6	**Aa**	**I See**
	Suggested Words	Suggested Words / High-Frequency Words
	acrobats, alligator, anthill, ants, apple	ambulance, ants, apple, astronaut I, see, the

Lesson		
7	**Tt**	**We Like Toys**
	Suggested Words	Suggested Words / High-Frequency Words
	teddy bear, tracks, train, triangle, trampolines, tree, turtle, turtles	tiger, tools, toys, truck, twins I, like, the, we

Lesson		
8	**Cc**	**I Can See**
	Suggested Words	Suggested Words / High-Frequency Words
	camel, camels, cap, carrots, cars, castle, cat, cats, clouds, computer	castle, cat, caterpillar, computer a, I, see

Lesson 9

Pp	I Like Animals	
Suggested Words	**Suggested Words**	**High-Frequency Words**
pajamas, pan, parachutes, pencils, penguins, pirouettes, pop, popcorn	pandas, parrots, pigs, polar bears	I, like, see, to

Lesson 10

Mmmm, Good!		The Playground	
Suggested Words	**High-Frequency Words**	**Suggested Words**	**High-Frequency Words**
apples, carrots, pumpkins, tomatoes	I, like, see, to, we	jump rope, slide, sprinkler, swings, water fountain	I, like, see, the, to, we

Unit 3

Lesson 11

Pat Cat, Sam Cat		Pam Cat	
Decodable Words	**High-Frequency Words**	**Decodable Words**	**High-Frequency Words**
Target Skill: Words with Short *a*	come, I, me, to	Target Skill: Words with Short *a*	and, come, I, me, see, to
am*, cat, Pat, Sam, sat		cat, Pam, pat, sat	

Lesson 12

I Can Nap		Tap with Me	
Decodable Words	**High-Frequency Words**	**Decodable Words**	**High-Frequency Words**
Target Skill: Words with *n*	I, my, with, we	Target Skill: Words with *n*	I, me, with
am*, can*, Dan, nap, Pat		am*, can*, man*, Nan, tap	

Lesson 13

Cam, Fan, Pam, and Mac		Fat Cat	
Decodable Words	**High-Frequency Words**	**Decodable Words**	**High-Frequency Words**
Target Skill: Words with *f* Cam, can*, cat, fan, fat, Mac, nap, Nat, Pam, pat, Sam, sat, tan	a, and, see, what, with, you	Target Skill: Words with *f* can*, cat, fat, Sam, sat, tap	a, see, the, to, what, you

Lesson 14

What Now?		Bab At Bat	
Decodable Words	**High-Frequency Words**	**Decodable Words**	**High-Frequency Words**
Target Skill: Words with *b* at*, Bab, bat, can*, Nan, nap, Nat, Pam, pat, Sam, tap	and, are, now, we, what	Target Skill: Words with *b* at*, Bab, bam, bat, can*, Pat	are, now, see, we, you

Lesson 15

Mac and Pam Cat		Come with Me	
Decodable Words	**High-Frequency Words**	**Decodable Words**	**High-Frequency Words**
Review Short *a, n, f, b* can*, cat, fan, Mac, Pam, pat, sat	and, come, me, to, with	Review Short *a, n, f, b* Bab, can*, Nan, Nat, sat	and, come, me, see, with

Photo Credits

Placement Key: (r) right, (l) left, (c) center, (t) top, (b) bottom, (bg) background

---